Baby Bat Bedtime

By Paige Towler and Smithsonian Bat Lab

Illustrated by Gavin Scott

Smithsonian kids

PUBLISHED by SLEEPING BEAR PRESS™

in collaboration with SMITHSONIAN INSTITUTION

At the end of a warm, dark night
in the rainforest, dawn began to break.
The sky turned pink and twinkly blue.

Down on the ground, furry animals were stirring and stretching.

But up in the tall trees, small brown bats were getting ready for sleep.

There were mama bats.
There were papa bats.
And there were baby bats!

One baby bat did not want to
get ready for bed.

She was not tired—
not even a little bit.

In fact, she was ready to stay up
the whole day! She wiggled her ears.
She fluttered her wings.
And she babbled excitedly: Eee-eee-eee!

Mama Bat chirped soothingly back at Baby:

Skree-skree-dee.

Then she called Baby
for a bedtime snack:

Skree-chee-chee.

Instead, Baby turned up her nose!
But Mama Bat knew what to do.

She swooped into the sky.
She looped above the trees
and scooped up a buzzing beetle.

She flew back to Baby Bat.

But Baby Bat still turned up her nose.
She wasn't hungry!

Mama Bat held the bug closer.

Well . . . maybe Baby was a *little* hungry.

CRUNCH!

Now Baby Bat's belly was nice and full.
She yawned, stretching her wings wide.

But she still wasn't ready for bed.
And she wasn't at all tired!
(Well, maybe a *tiny* bit. But that was it!)

Now it was time for a bat bath.

Baby tried to wriggle away.

Who needed baths when there
was playing to do?

But Mama Bat knew what to do.
She gently held Baby Bat still.
She stuck out her pink tongue.
She licked Baby Bat all over,

from Baby's batty ears . . .

to her batty nose . . .

to her batty toes.

Baby relaxed.
She felt cozy and warm.
Her fur was soft and clean.

Hmmm . . .
maybe baths were pretty nice.

Baby Bat yawned, stretching out her pink tongue. Her head drooped a bit.

But she still wasn't *that* tired.

Mama scooped Baby up to her soft, warm chest.
Baby held on tight.
Using her strong wings, Mama rose into the early sky.

Together they swooped and looped in the warm air.
The movement rocked Baby side to side.
A gentle breeze blew through her fur.

After a while, Mama landed on
the trunk of a nearby tree.

Mama held Baby upside down, nice and snug.

Around them, other bats began to sing:

Skree-skree-dee,
skree-chee-chee!

Baby Bat babbled along. Mama Bat cooed back:
Skree-chee-chee!

Baby Bat was clean and cozy.
The air was warm and calm.
Mama Bat's fur was thick and soft.
Baby listened to Mama Bat softly coo.
But still, she wasn't that . . .

Zzzzzzz . . .

Short-tailed fruit bats cuddle close together.

All About Bats!

At first bats and humans might seem very different. But bats do a lot of the same things people do! Just like humans, bats need to get ready for bed. They eat good meals so they have full bellies, and take baths so they are clean. Baby bats also have family members who take care of them and give them cuddles. In fact, just like little humans, baby bats even practice talking by babbling! How do we know all of this? It is all thanks to bat scientists: people who study real-life bats.

The Smithsonian Tropical Research Institute, Gamboa Lab

Let's Meet the Real Bat Scientists!

Most nights, several scientists wander deep into the jungles of Panama looking for something very important to them . . . bats!

Gamboa, Panama

These scientists work and study at the Smithsonian Bat Lab, which is part of the Smithsonian Tropical Research Institute, in Panama. Led by principal investigator Dr. Rachel Page, this team studies bats in the wild. Bats are a very important part of something called the ecosystem.

Two white-throated round-eared bats in Panama eating their favorite prey – katydids!

An **ecosystem** is an area where living things—like plants, animals, and more—interact with each other and with the environment.

Many bats eat insects. This is good for the environment. Without bats, there would be too many insects eating all the plants. When bats eat insects, it helps keep the local ecosystem healthy and balanced.

A Jamaican fruit bat collecting fruit.

Some bats only eat insects. Others eat small animals like frogs and fish. Other bats are vegetarian: they eat fruit, seeds, and more. After a bat eats fruit or seeds, the seeds come out in the bat's waste. Now a new plant can grow from the seeds. Bats that eat fruit and seeds are called **seed dispersers**. These bats are the farmers of the forest, spreading seeds that grow into new plants.

Bat poop is also called **guano**.

Bats that eat **nectar**—a sugary liquid made by plants—are also very important to the ecosystem. These bats are **pollinators**. Many kinds of plants need something called **pollen** to reproduce—or create more plants. In order for these plants to reproduce, pollen from the male plant must travel to a female plant. That's where bats come in!

A **seed disperser** *is something that spreads seeds into new places where they may grow. Some animals—like fruit-eating bats—do this when they dine on fruit and then later poop out the seeds in a new place.*

When this leaf-nosed bat eats a fruit's seeds, it will later spread these seeds in its guano—or poop.

A **pollinator** is an animal that helps plants reproduce by bringing pollen from one plant to another.

When a bat visits a male flower to eat, the bat gets covered in the plant's pollen. Then the hungry bat visits another flower. Because the bat is covered in pollen from the first flower, it accidentally leaves some of the pollen behind. If this second flower is female, it now has the pollen it needs to make more plants!

A leaf-nosed bat dines on the nectar of a flower.

Bat scientists at the Smithsonian Tropical Research Institute learn about how bats help the ecosystem. The information the team learns helps them understand bats better. It also lets them make sure the bats are healthy. This keeps the environment healthy, too. The scientists also use the information they learn to teach people around the world about bats. When more and more people care about bats, more people can work to protect them and keep them safe!

How to Study Bats

To study bats, the scientists must be very patient. They also need to be careful not to disturb the bats. Take a look at some of the special tools scientists in the Smithsonian Bat Lab use to learn about bats.

Dr. Fernandez uses an ultrasonic microphone to record the sounds bats make.

Recording Devices

Scientists use ultrasonic microphones to record bats in action. These devices can record very high-pitched sounds—sounds that are way higher than humans can normally hear. Scientists can use these recordings to learn how bats communicate with each other, find their food, and stay safe from other animals.

Mist Nets

A mist net is a type of soft net that scientists set up in the forest. These nets let researchers safely capture bats without hurting them. The scientists watch and study the bats, and then release them back into the wild.

Mist nets can catch bats like this leaf-nosed bat without hurting them. Later, after scientists study the bats, they release the bats back into the wild.

Dr. Page uses a headlamp to study bats when it is dark out.

Headlamps

Many scientists study bats at night when bats are most active. Bats use something called **echolocation** to find their way at night. But the scientists need help to see in the dark! Bat scientists wear special flashlights on their heads that let them keep their hands free.

Bat Guano

By studying a bat's poop, scientists can learn what a bat ate and how healthy it is.

Echolocation *is a process that some animals use to find their way around—and to find food—by sending out high-pitched sounds and listening to how these noises bounce off objects.*

Greater Sac-Winged Bats

There are many kinds of bats in the world (more than 1,450 different species worldwide!). The type of bats in the story you just read are called greater sac-winged bats, *Saccopteryx bilineata*. These are small bats that live in Central and South America.

Scientists working at the Smithsonian have found that—just like in the story—greater sac-winged bats have interesting behaviors—many of which may be similar to yours!

A greater sac-winged bat mom holds her pup close.

Dr. Fernandez uses a mist net to safely capture a greater sac-winged bat.

Bat Babbling

Do baby bats really babble? Yes! At the Smithsonian Bat Lab, a team of scientists led by Dr. Ahana Fernandez discovered that baby bats babble just like human babies do.

While studying greater sac-winged baby bats, known as pups, Dr. Fernandez and her advisor, Dr. Mirjam Knörnschild, learned that bat pups often copy the sounds adult bats make by using a type of "babbling." Then Dr. Fernandez noticed something else—the bat parents call back! They use a form of "baby talk" to speak to their pups, something the scientists sometimes call "motherese."

Dr. Fernandez uses gloves to safely hold a small bat.

Dr. Fernandez records the sounds made by greater sac-winged bats.

Dr. Knörnschild watches a greater sac-winged bat flying.

Smithsonian

Greater sac-winged bats are known for singing bat songs to attract mates and tell others where their home is. Babbling helps the pups practice singing!

Dr. Fernandez discovered that bat "babbling" is very similar to the way human babies babble. Babbling helps human babies learn to speak. The same is likely true for bat pups: babbling—and having bat moms use baby talk in return—seems to help the pups learn to communicate like the grown-ups! And, for both humans and bats, this babbling and baby talk may also help parents and their babies bond.

Aside from songbirds and humans, bats are the only animals known to use baby talk with their babies while the babies are learning to communicate.

A greater sac-winged bat pup holds tight to her mom's chest.

Greater sac-winged bats sing and call while perching on a tree.

A sleepy greater sac-winged bat pup yawns!

More Bat Behavior

Families are important to bats. Greater sac-winged bats live in the jungle in groups called colonies, made up of about 15 to 20 bats.

Like human babies, bat pups drink milk from their moms for the first part of their lives. When a bat pup is born, she will cling to her mom's chest. Bat moms will sometimes hunt for food while flying with pups on their chests. Other times, they drop the pups off in a safe spot.

Bats are nocturnal, which usually means that they sleep during the day and wake up at night. However, greater sac-winged bats don't need much sleep. Even during the day, they spend time together singing and babbling. Like all bats, greater sac-winged bats hang upside down when they are not flying—even when they're sleeping!

How to Help Bats

Greater sac-winged bats live in Central and South America—including in Panama, near the Smithsonian Bat Lab.

Greater sac-winged bats aren't the only bats, though—there are more than 1,450 species of bats around the world. Some of them may live in or near your neighborhood!

Here are some ways you can help protect the bats that live near you.

Grow a Night Garden

If you have outdoor space available, have an adult help you plant night-scented flowers—flowers that bloom and give off their scents at night—native to your area. This can provide nectar for bats to eat. Your garden will also attract insects, which are a yummy snack for more than 70 percent of all bat species.

Avoid Pesticides

If you have a garden or lawn, ask your family to avoid using chemicals called pesticides.

Keep Cats Indoors at Night

Cats are excellent hunters—which can mean trouble for bats! Keeping cats inside at night helps keep bats safe.

Be a Bat Buddy

Share your love of bats with friends and family! Teach others that not only do bats play really important roles in our ecosystems, they are also amazing animals with many interesting behaviors—just like us!

To learn more about bats and the scientists who study them, see the Smithsonian Bat Lab website: noseleaf.org. You can learn more about baby bat babbling, and bat communication in general, by visiting mirjam-knoernschild.org. To discover more about fieldwork in the tropics, visit the Smithsonian Tropical Research Institute website: stri.si.edu.

To my mom, who's always known just what to do.
—PT

To Elisabeth Kalko, bat researcher extraordinaire who inspired so much passion, curiosity, and
scientific inquiry in generations of tropical bat researchers. Her inspiration lives in our hearts.
And to the bats of the Panamanian rainforest—thank you for sharing your stories with us!
—Smithsonian Bat Lab

For Finnen
—GS

Smithsonian kids

The Smithsonian name and logo are registered trademarks of the Smithsonian.

For Smithsonian Enterprises:
Avery Naughton, Licensing Coordinator; Paige Towler, author and Editorial Lead; Jill Corcoran,
Senior Director of Licensed Publishing; Brigid Ferraro, Vice President of New Business and Licensing; Carol LeBlanc, President

For Smithsonian Bat Lab:
Rachel Page, Smithsonian Staff Scientist and Director of Smithsonian Bat Lab, Panama; Ahana Fernandez, Postdoctoral Researcher at the Museum of Natural History in Berlin, Germany, and
visiting postdoc at the Smithsonian Tropical Research Institute, Panama; Mirjam Knörnschild, Professor for Evolutionary Ethology at the Humboldt University and the Museum for Natural
History in Berlin, Germany, and Research Associate at the Smithsonian Tropical Research Institute, Panama; Gregg Cohen, Manager of the Smithsonian Bat Lab, Panama

For Smithsonian Tropical Research Institute, Office of Communications:
Linette Dutari, Associate Director, Lina González, Design Supervisor,
Jorge Alemán, Graphic Design Specialist, Beth King, Communications Manager,
Sonia Tejada, Local Press Writer, Leila Nilipour, Copywriter, Vanessa Crooks, Writer and Publishing Specialist,
Ana Endara, Videographer, Paulette Guardia, Graphic Design Specialist

SLEEPING BEAR PRESS™

2395 South Huron Parkway, Suite 200, Ann Arbor, MI 48104
www.sleepingbearpress.com • © Sleeping Bear Press
Manufactured in the United States
10 9 8 7 6 5 4 3 2 1
Library of Congress Cataloging-in-Publication Data
Names: Towler, Paige, author. | Smithsonian Institution, contributor. | Scott, Gavin, illustrator.
Title: Baby bat bedtime / by Paige Towler and Smithsonian Institution ; illustrated by Gavin Scott.
Description: Ann Arbor, MI : Sleeping Bear Press, [2024] | Audience: Ages 4-8 | Summary: "As dawn starts to rise in the rainforest, animals are
waking up. But some animals are going to bed instead. Small brown bats have been busy all night; now it's time for them to settle in among the
trees. But one baby bat wants to stay up and play"-- Provided by publisher.
Identifiers: LCCN 2024005270 | ISBN 9781534113220 (hardcover) | Subjects: LCSH: Little brown bat--Behavior--Juvenile literature. |
Nocturnal animals--Behavior--Juvenile literature. | Classification: LCC QL737.C595 T69 2024 | DDC 599.415--dc23/eng/20240405
LC record available at https://lccn.loc.gov/2024005270 | ISBN 9781534113220
Photo Credits: Gregg Cohen, Rachel Page, Steve Paton, Claudia Rahlmeier, Andreas Rose, Imran Razik, Simon Ripperger, Michael Stifter, Christian Ziegler